First published in the U.S. in 1989 by Ideals Publishing Corporation,
Nashville, Tennesee 37214

Printed and bound by MacLehose & Partners Ltd, United Kingdom

Library of Congress Cataloging-in-Publication Data

McCaughrean, Geraldine.
       The story of Noah and the ark / by Geraldine McCaughrean ;
illustrated by Helen Ward.
              p.   cm.
       Summary: Before He floods the earth, God tells Noah to build an
ark and take two of every animal on board.
       ISBN 0-8249-8403-X
       1. Noah's ark—Juvenile literature.   2. Noah (Biblical figure)—
—Juvenile literature.   3. Deluge—Juvenile literature.   4. Bible
stories, English—O.T. Genesis.   [1. Noah (Biblical figure)
2. Noah's ark.   3. Bible stories—O.T.]   I. Ward, Helen, 1962-
ill.   II. Title.
BS658.M35   1989
222'.11092—dc20   89-7599
                                                                      CIP
                                                                      AC

THE STORY OF

NOAH AND THE ARK

story by Geraldine McCaughrean
pictures by Helen Ward

IDEALS CHILDREN'S BOOKS
Nashville, Tennessee

There was a time, on a day rather like today, when God looked out over the earth and shook his head and sighed. All he could see was unkindness and greed and selfishness.

"Men are so wicked," said God, "all except Noah. They have forgotten me entirely and I'm sorry I ever created them. If it weren't for Noah and the animals, I would . . . I would . . ."

The angels trembled to see God so angry, and the sky held its breath.

Noah was a good carpenter and a good man. He lived with his family between two rivers. Every day he thanked God for his life and his wife and his three sons, Shem, Ham, and Japheth.

One day while Noah was working at his bench, singing a jolly song, a loud voice rolled out of the hills:

"Noah! Noah! Build me an ark!"

Noah looked up from his work, but he could see no one – nothing but the sun sinking between the hills and the dust gusting across the fields. Noah's heart thumped and his saw trembled in his hand. He cleared his throat nervously and said, "An ark, Lord?"

"Yes, Noah. Build me a boat three stories high. Gather into it every kind of animal that walks or crawls or runs upon the earth. For I have decided to send a flood, and I could not bear to see you or the animals drown."

"What are you making, Husband?" asked
Noah's wife when she saw him hammering.

"I'm building a boat," said Noah.

"A boat? All this way from the sea?" asked his wife.

"It's going to rain," said Noah, and he went on
hammering.

"What are you building, Father?" asked Noah's
sons when they saw him cutting wood.

"I'm building an ark," said Noah.

"An ark, Father? All this way from
the sea?" asked his sons.

"It's going to rain," said Noah, and
he went on sawing.

"What are you doing, old man?" jeered the neighbors, throwing stones at Noah's ark.

"I'm building a ship," said Noah.

"Building a ship?" laughed the neighbors. "All this way from the sea? Ha ha ha!"

"It's going to rain," said Noah quietly.

But his neighbors just held out their hands, looked up at the cloudless sky, and snorted with laughter.

As Noah banged in the last nail, his two dogs jumped up and ran into the ark.

"Ah, I see it is time to fetch the animals," said Noah, laying aside his tools.

First he gathered in all the gentle animals – two of each kind, one male and one female. Two by two they went into the ark: pigeons and pandas, marmots and mice, squirrels and sheep, lemurs and lemmings, oxen and ostriches, a cow and two cats, horses and hamsters and deer and donkeys.

Next he gathered in all the fierce, ferocious animals – one male and one female: lions and lynxes, tigers and tarantulas, hogs and hyenas, panthers and pumas, two bears and a bull, jackals and jaguars, foxes and ferrets, stoats and scorpions, weasels and wildcats and wolves.

Then Noah gathered in all the slithering, sliding, creeping, crawling, and writhing creatures – two of each kind, one male and one female. Two by two they went into the ark: snails and slugs, anacondas and alligators, crabs and caterpillars and lizards too.

He gathered into the ark all the animals in the world, however big or small. When the hippopotamuses arrived, the gangplank creaked. When the elephants arrived, the whole ark shook.

"The ark is almost full, but there's still room for you," said Noah when the smallest creatures arrived: the bugs and the bats, the mites and the mosquitoes, the worms and woodlice and weevils.

While Noah found room on the ark for all of God's creatures, Shem, Ham, and Japheth fetched food and water and straw. Then, just as two tortoises were creeping slowly up the gangplank, a drop of rain splashed onto Noah's nose.

"Shem. Ham. Japheth. Fetch your wives and plenty of food. We must all go into the ark now," said Noah. So Shem, Ham, and Japheth fetched their wives and plenty of food and went into the ark.

Mrs. Noah was chatting with her neighbor when Noah called, "Wife! It's time to go."

"Do we really have to go into the ark and sleep with all those animals?" asked Mrs. Noah.

"Yes, we do," said Noah. And they too went into the ark.

The rain fell in big, startling drops. *Splash! Splash*! Clouds bounded like sheep across the sky. Thunder growled behind the hills. And lightning made midnight as bright as day.

Drifting rain as thick as waving grass filled up the space between the sky and the earth. Noah pulled up the gangplank, and God shut the door of the ark.

"Noah! Noah! The water is up to our ankles!" shouted his neighbors. "Open the door!"

"Noah! Noah! The water is up to our waists! Let down the gangplank!"

"Noah! Noah! The water is up to our necks! We should have listened to you! Let us in!"

But Noah could not hear them above the drumming of the rain.

The rain beat down. Little by little, the lapping
water covered the grass and bushes; and
crickets and grasshoppers took shelter on the
roof of the ark.

Little by little, the lapping water covered the
hills and mountains too. It blotted out the earth.

From one horizon to another, there was nothing but water. As far as the eye could see, there was nothing but water.

The only sound was the creaking of the ark – and the roaring, mewing, growling, purring, barking, cheeping, squawking, squeaking, mooing, and chewing of the animals and birds – and the chattering of Noah's family.

The rain hung like the folds of a cloak across the sky. For forty days and forty nights, it rained. Sometimes the dark shape of a whale passed by on the horizon, or a porpoise leapt along beneath the bow of the boat. But otherwise Noah's family and the animals drifted alone across the great expanse of water.

Far below, the earth that God had once given to his ungrateful people was given now to the octopuses and the sharks, the eels and the rays, and a million other strange fish.

Then the rain stopped drumming on the roof, and the clouds disappeared, and the roof of the ark steamed in the sun.

For a hundred and fifty days, the sun shone on the water, drying it up. But still no speck of land was uncovered. The animals' food was all used up, and the lions looked hungrily at the wildebeests, and the hawks turned a beady eye on the mice.

Noah took a raven on his wrist and opened a window of the ark. He threw the raven up into the air and watched it flap away across the waves. It disappeared into the crack between the sky and the sea and never came back.

Noah then took a dove to the window and threw it up into the sky. It flew this way and that across the water, searching for food. The next day it returned, weary and drooping with hunger.

Noah stroked the dove. "So the earth is still covered, is it, my friend? We must wait a little longer."

After seven more days, Noah threw the other dove up into the sky. It flew this way and that, to and fro, and they lost sight of it against the brightness of the sky.

Then Shem, Ham, and Japheth called to their wives: "Look! Look! The dove has returned, and there is something in its mouth!"

Noah caught the dove and found a fresh twig from an olive tree held tightly in its beak. "So you found dry land, did you, my friend? Then it's time for you and your mate to fly there and build a nest."

During the next seven days, all the wasps and flies and butterflies and moths and all the birds sprang up off the roof of the ark and flew away. The trees were above the water now, and there were nests to be built.

The next day at noon there came a terrible grating crash. The whole ark lurched, and the animals tumbled together in a heap. The ark had run aground!

Its hull was wedged in the forked peak of a mountain called Ararat. By morning, the sodden mountain slopes were laid bare, and Noah's ark hung balanced in the sky.

Noah unfastened the door and ran down the gangplank. Two by two the animals left the ark and picked their ways down the steep and muddy paths.

The springboks sprang into the far distance, and the lions bounded after them. The monkeys climbed into the trees, and the alligators plunged nose-first into the swollen rivers. The mongooses and the snakes stared at one another in the sun. The camels headed toward the desert, and the sea lions started the long journey south. When all the other animals had gone, the tortoises started slowly down the gangplank.

Then Noah called together his sons and his sons' wives and he said, "We are the only people left in the world. You and your children and your children's children must start afresh. Where will you go?"

"South," said Shem, "where the sun is hot."

"I shall go north," said Ham, "where the light won't hurt my eyes and the sun won't scorch my skin."

"And I shall go east," said Japheth, "and have many children in the land where the sun rises. But what will you do, Father?"

"Oh, I shall settle here and grow grapes and sit under my vines with Mrs. Noah and grow old . . . But first there is something very important I must do!"

And with that, Noah built an altar to God and offered a sacrifice to him.

"Now let us say a prayer to God," said Noah, "to praise and thank him for saving our lives. Shem. Ham. Japheth. Don't forget to tell your children about why God sent the flood. Tell them to be good people and to remember God night and morning and not to make him sad or angry ever again."

Sadly, Noah and his wife waved good-bye to their sons and the wives of their sons.

"But what if they *aren't* such good people as you, Husband?" asked Mrs. Noah. "Will God send another flood and another and another, so that they have to begin over and over again?"

A drop of rain fell into Noah's eye. He wiped it away as if it were a tear.

"God must know best, my dear."

"*Don't worry, Noah. Don't fret, Mrs. Noah.*"

They looked around, but could see no one.

"I give you my promise, Noah," said God. "There shall be no more floods sent to destroy the earth. I shall write that promise in the sky, in language everyone will understand. You shall see it there whenever rainclouds start to break!"

Noah looked up, and there in the sky was an arc of color – all the colors known to man – bending like a bridge between heaven and earth.

The sign, a token of God's promise, was a rainbow.

The end